# Beginners Guide to Tab

Introduction 3

1. The Stave 4

2. Additional Note Information 8
   Staccato 9
   Glissando 10
   Tremolo Strumming 11
   Tremolo Arm Vibrato 12
   String Bends 13
   String Bends & Vibrato 18
   Musical Ornaments - 'hammer-ons' and 'pull-offs' 19
   Raking 23
   Harmonics 24
   Artificial Harmonics 25

10 'Til 2 (play-along track) 26

Musical Terms 32

**Wise Publications**
London / New York / Paris / Sydney / Copenhagen / Madrid

Exclusive Distributors:
Music Sales Limited
8/9 Frith Street, London W1V 5TZ, England.
Music Sales Pty Limited
120 Rothschild Avenue, Rosebery, NSW 2018, Australia.

Order No. AM91099
ISBN 0-7119-3430-4
This book © Copyright 1994 by Wise Publications.

Unauthorised reproduction of any part of
this publication by any means including photocopying
is an infringement of copyright.

Cover designed by Michael Bell Design.
Compiled by Arthur Dick.
Music processed by The Pitts.

Your Guarantee of Quality:
As publishers, we strive to produce every book to the highest commercial standards.
Throughout, the printing and binding have been planned to
ensure a sturdy, attractive publication which should give years of enjoyment.
If your copy fails to meet our high standards, please inform us and we will gladly replace it.

Music Sales' complete catalogue describes thousands of
titles and is available in full colour sections by subject, direct from Music Sales Limited.
Please state your areas of interest and send a cheque/postal order for £1.50 for postage to:
Music Sales Limited, Newmarket Road, Bury St. Edmunds, Suffolk IP33 3YB.

Printed in the United Kingdom by
Caligraving Limited, Thetford, Norfolk.

# Beginner's Guide to Tab

## Introduction

Wouldn't it be wonderful to transform what you see written on a piece of music onto the guitar fretboard and make the music come to life by including all the phrases and nuances associated with the piece. Tablature (TAB) helps you to do this. It is not a replacement for standard musical notation, it is simply a pictorial version of the music displayed on a guitar fretboard!

If you have ever seen TAB notation you may have wondered what all the numbers and arrows really mean and how they should be interpreted.

This book and accompanying cassette starts at the beginning and shows you, step by step, what each TAB instruction refers to. The instructions are demonstrated on the cassette.

But let's start at the beginning!

## 1. The Stave

The stave is a set of lines and spaces each representing a pitch, on which music is written.

The music stave is drawn as five lines with a Treble Clef at the beginning of each line. The notes above and below the stave are shown on **leger** lines. For example, the six open strings of the guitar are notated as follows.

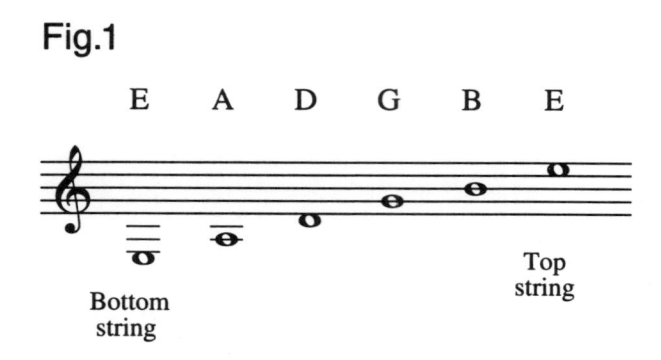

Fig.1

Bottom string

Top string

The thickest string is the 6th string. It is shown on the music as the note E, below the stave. It is considered as the **bottom** string because it is drawn as the bottom line on the TAB diagram. (Fig. 2.) The next string is A, the 5th string, then D the 4th string, G the 3rd string, B the 2nd and E the 1st or **top** string.

Throughout this book the right hand is considered the 'pick' or 'plectrum' hand and the left is the 'fret' hand. Pictorially, (sorry if you're left handed – you will have to turn the diagram around!) the guitar neck is viewed from above as if you are looking down on the fretboard.

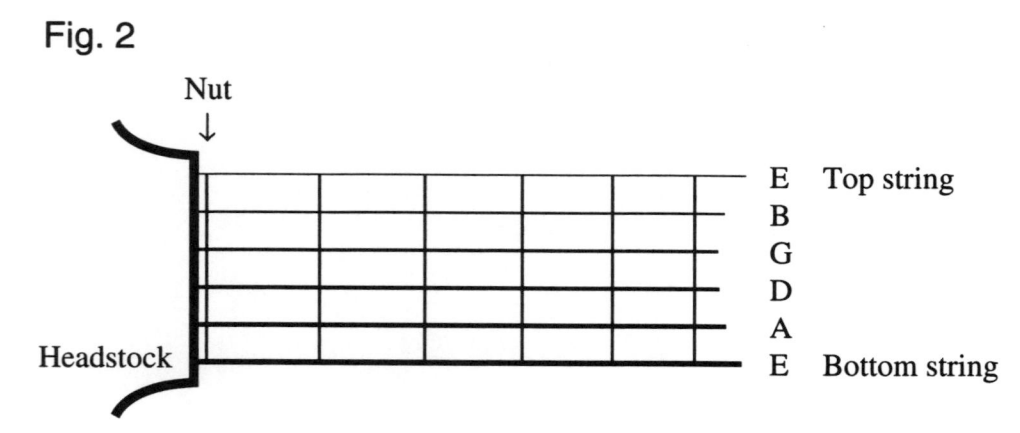

Fig. 2

Nut

Headstock

E Top string
B
G
D
A
E Bottom string

It is from this pictorial representation that TAB comes about. **The TAB 'stave' is a horizontal representation of the 6 guitar strings viewed from this perspective.** The position of the headstock and nut are taken as read and not usually shown as part of the TAB stave. This leaves only the six lines representing the six strings of the guitar with the lowest string (low E) as the bottom line and the top string (high E) as the top line.

To tell you which note to play on any given string, a number is placed on the corresponding line of the TAB. Each number refers to a **fret position**, e.g. F on the third leger line below the stave translates to '1' on the bottom line of the TAB. This means placing your finger on the space on the 6th string between the nut and the 1st fret.

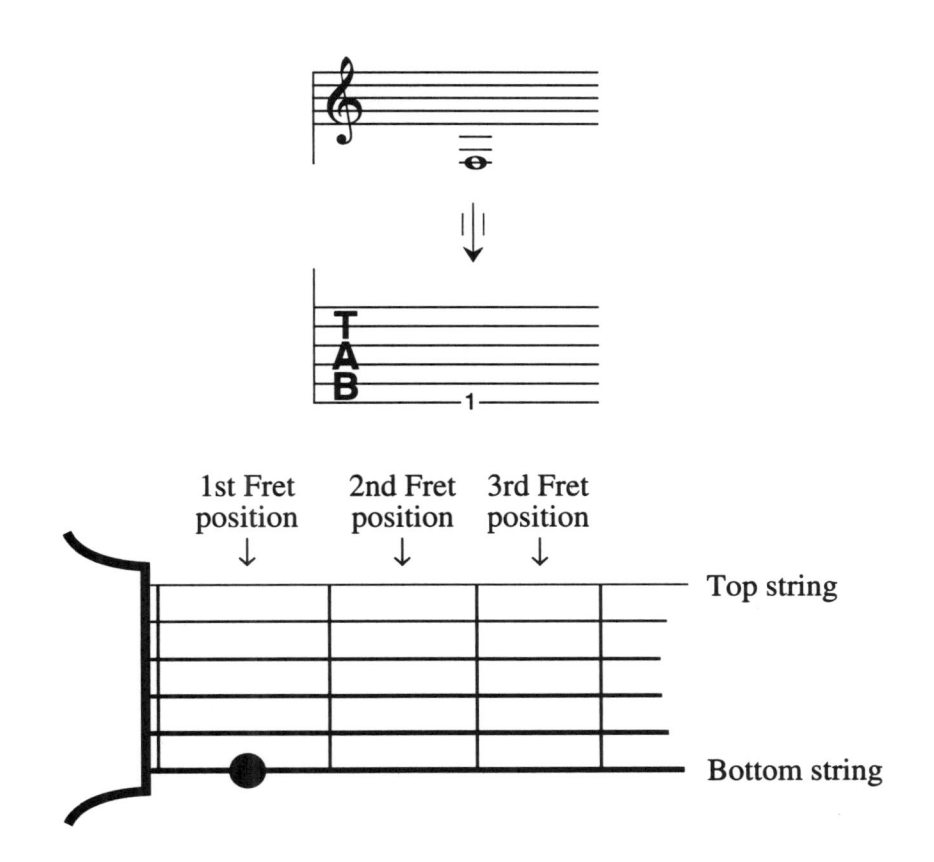

The TAB stave is always written directly underneath the music stave. Each number (i.e. fret position) on the TAB corresponds to a musical note vertically above on the music stave.

For example, the open strings of the guitar are written on the music stave and their corresponding TAB equivalents are written directly underneath.

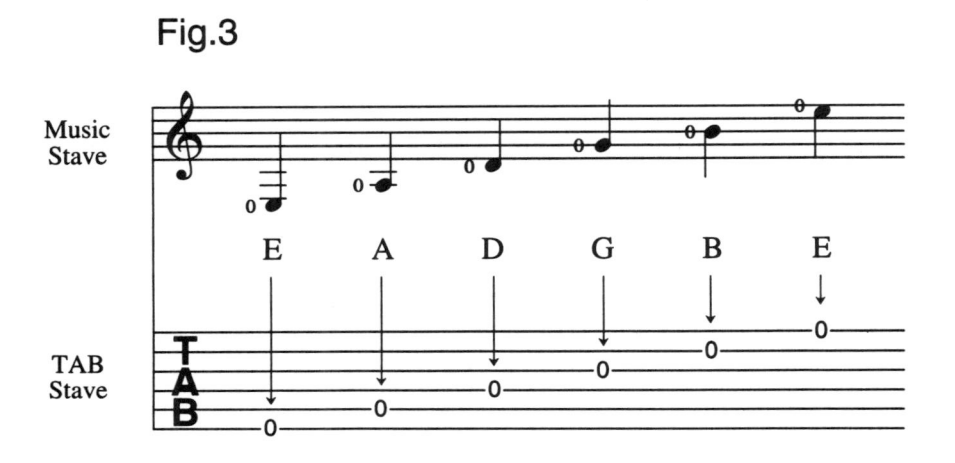

Fig.3

A zero is used to denote an open string on the TAB. (On the music stave a small o is sometimes placed to the left of the note to indicate an open string as opposed to the fretted equivalent.)

With this method we can designate the string and fret position for any note on the music stave.

When two notes are played together they are displayed vertically on both staves. Similarly with chords (3 notes or more); what you see on the music stave visually translates to the number on TAB. The following example should help make this clear.

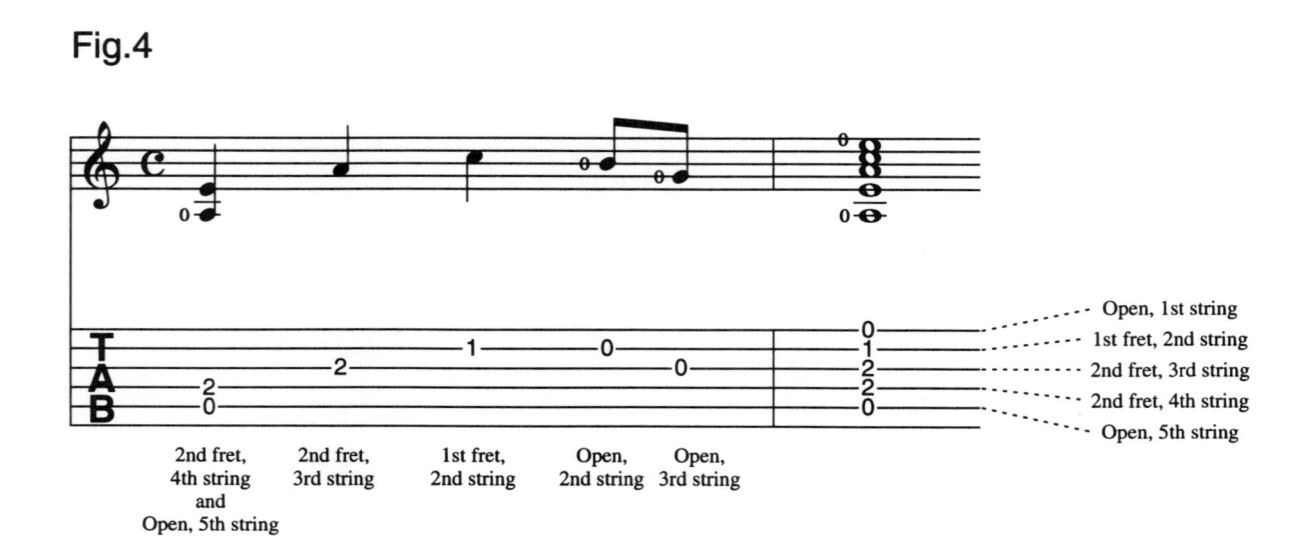

Fig.4

```
2nd fret,        2nd fret,     1st fret,    Open,        Open,
4th string       3rd string    2nd string   2nd string   3rd string
and
Open, 5th string
```

- - - Open, 1st string
- - - 1st fret, 2nd string
- - - 2nd fret, 3rd string
- - - 2nd fret, 4th string
- - - Open, 5th string

There are two instructions missing from the TAB notation which are necessary to produce the perfect performance! Firstly, the fingering detail (left hand in this case) – which fingers do I use to press the strings down onto the frets? And secondly, rhythm notation, which refers to the time values of the notes within each bar.

Firstly, the fingering problem…

Some music (notably classical pieces) will provide suggested left hand fingering but more often than not you have to work out what is most comfortable and logical.

In the previous example (Fig. 4) the two bars are best played using the following left hand fingering. (Try alternative fingering to see which is the most suitable if you are unsure.)

Fig.5

Sometimes it is not always obvious or even particularly important. It is up to you and your preferred choice. The next example shows two fingering patterns for the same phrase (the TAB of course is the same for both).

Fig.6

Musically the note is tied across the bar.

In TAB only the point at which the note is first struck is shown.

The second instruction, the time value of each note, is not directed from TAB.

Although the TAB clearly defines the note which is to be played on the fretboard, you have to look above to the music stave to understand the precise note value and rhythm of the phrase you are playing. There is no short cut, the TAB gives no time value to any of the notes.

If you are playing a part that has been transcribed from a recording then of course you can listen to the musical phrase and its precise rhythm for yourself.

## 2. Additional Note Information

There are many musical instructions which can be given to a note or group of notes, some of which are quite specific and others which are open to interpretation by you. Let's look at some in detail. All the following examples are illustrated on the cassette.

8va is written above the music stave and indicates that the notes that follow should be played an **octave higher** than written. 15va indicates a 2 octave transposition.

**loco** cancels the above instruction.

Note the following:

### Example 1

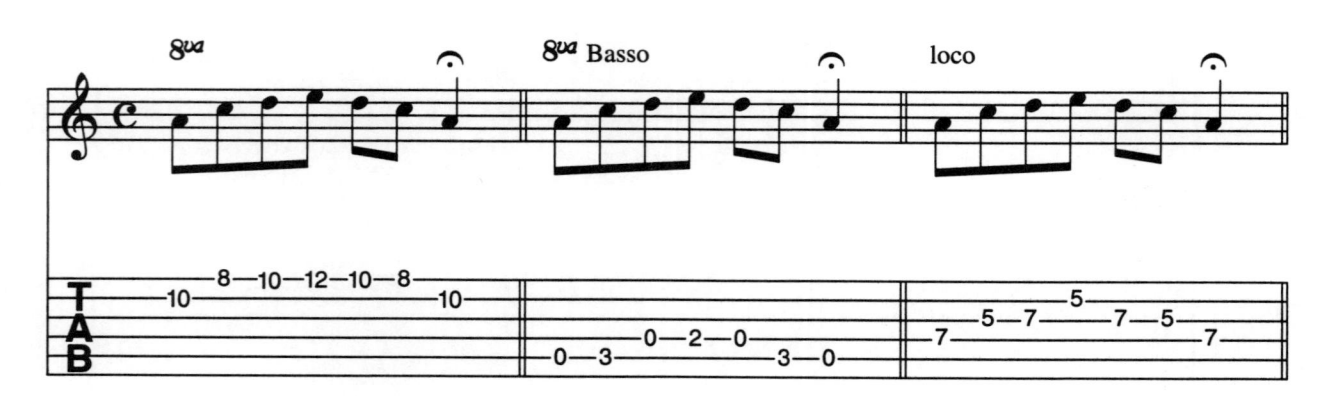

The TAB shows the note positions played up an octave;

The TAB shows the note positions played down an octave;

loco cancels the 8va instruction - the TAB changes accordingly.

**Staccato** (meaning 'detached') shortens the note. It is indicated by a dot over the note. To clarify the difference between long and short notes in a phrase a line is placed over the long notes.

### Example 2
Unaltered note lengths

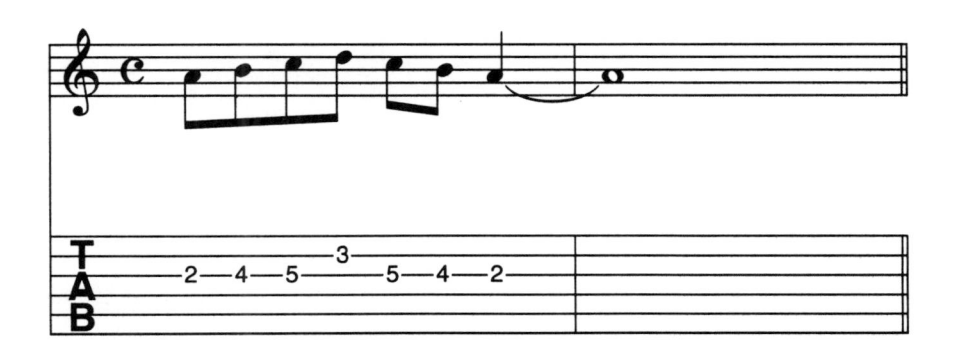

### Example 3
Staccato – Shortened note lengths

### Example 4
Mixture of long and short note lengths

Note: The TAB is the same for all these examples.

**Glissando** *abbr.* Gliss. Strike the note then slide your finger up or down the fretboard as indicated.

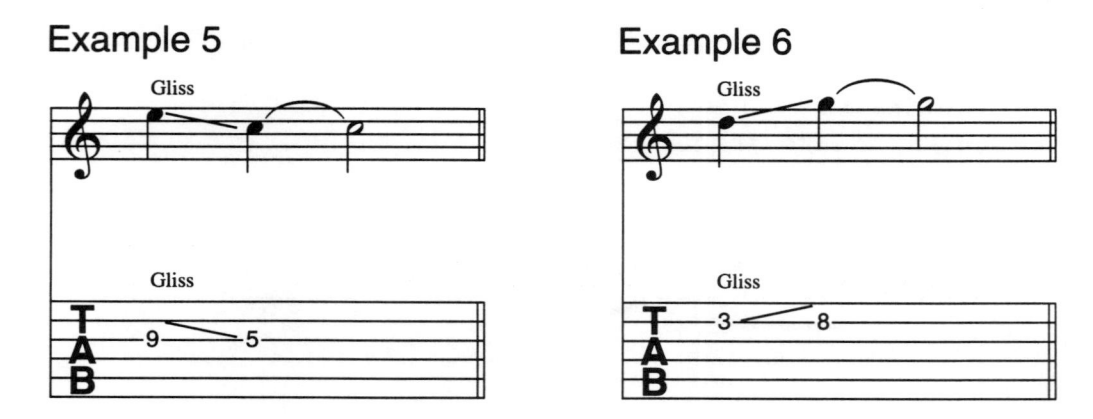

Example 5

Example 6

The glissando instruction is shown linking two notes, i.e. sliding down from E to C in the first instance or from D up to G in the second. In each case the first note is struck but the second sounds without being hit. The glissando can be used to slide a note 'off the fretboard' or used to indicate sliding up to a note from a non-specific point.

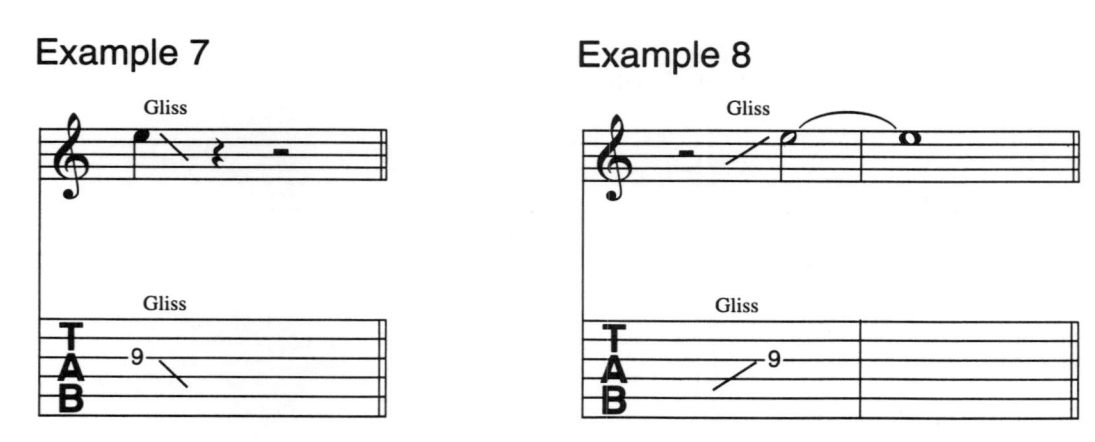

Example 7

Example 8

If the second note is struck it is notated with the symbol (▶) over it. The difference in effect can be heard by comparing the next two phrases.

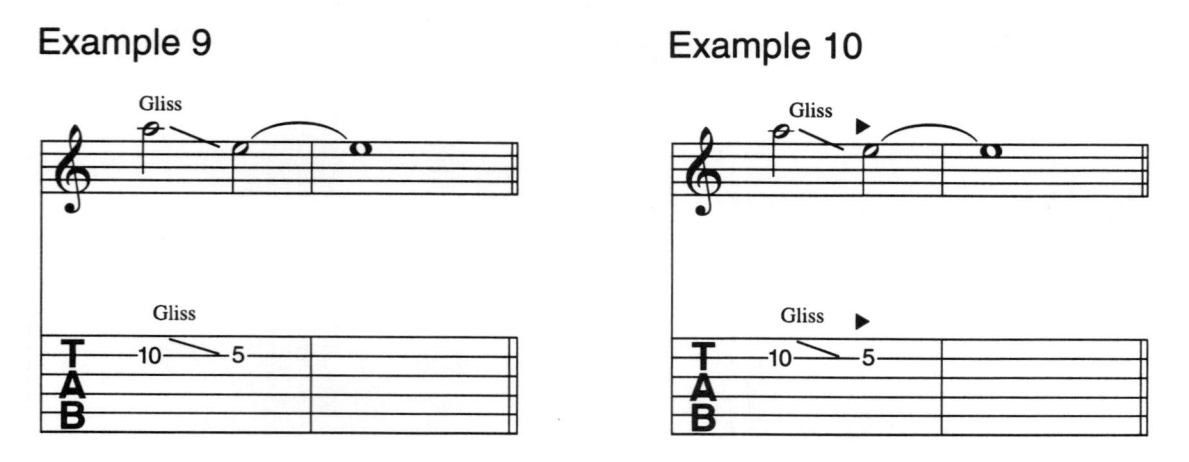

Example 9

Example 10

**Tremolo Strumming** is indicated by marking the note(s) in the following manner.

Example 11

This requires the note(s) to be struck in a fast succession of up and down strokes (i.e. as fast as possible).

**Finger Vibrato** (vib.) literally means 'shaking' the note with your finger and is indicated on the music by placing a wavy line over the note.

The rapid but minute fluctuations in pitch give an expressive quality to the note. The precise amount of vibrato is left entirely to the discretion of the performer. The use of vibrato in jazz, blues and rock music is especially noticeable where the effect becomes a characteristic trademark of the performer's style.

In the following examples compare the sound with and without vibrato and the effect created by delaying its use.

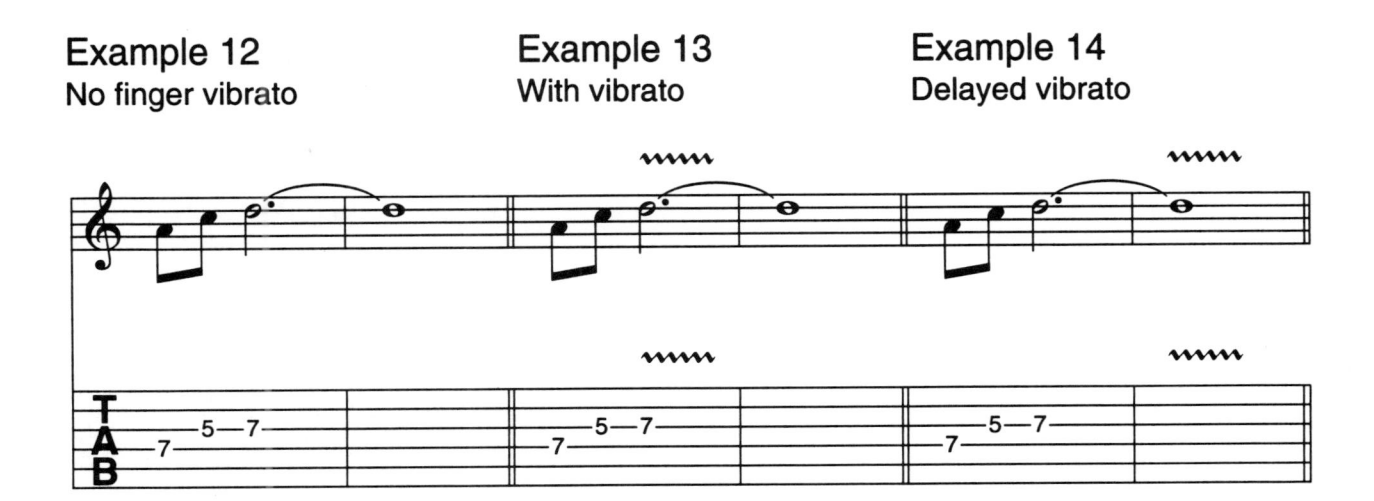

Example 12
No finger vibrato

Example 13
With vibrato

Example 14
Delayed vibrato

**Tremolo Arm Vibrato**

By varying the movement of the tremolo arm (or whammy bar) a vibrato effect can be created. The more the arm is depressed the greater the depth of vibrato. Again, the amount of expression created by the arm movement is not easy to display on the music and is left to the performer's discretion.

Example 15

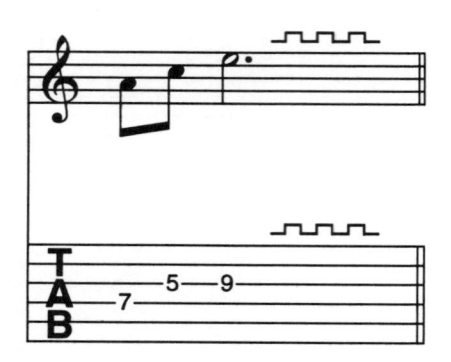

The tremolo arm can be used for other effects. A 'dive bomb' is created by striking the note(s) and simultaneously depressing the arm to drop the pitch to an indefinite point. The arm can also be used to create bends up to a note, i.e strike the note with the arm depressed and then release, bringing the note up to pitch. The interval of the bend is shown next to the tremolo arm symbol. Each ½ tone is equivalent to a 1 fret interval. 1½ tones is equivalent to a 3 fret interval. Pulling the tremolo arm upwards would be shown with a + marking. Listen to the following examples.

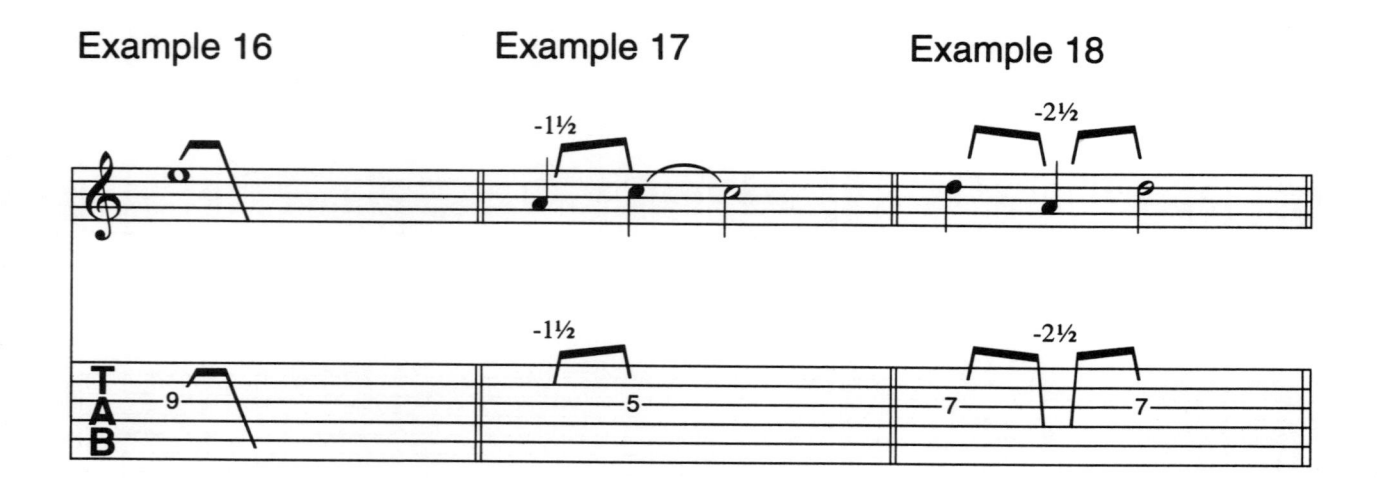

Example 16    Example 17    Example 18

**String Bends** and other musical ornaments.

Vibrato and string bends give the performer an almost infinite palette of expression. The precise amount depends upon the musical situation. In classical guitar music, for instance, string bending is not normally a feature, whereas in blues and rock playing it is very much part of the style.

The most common way of bending a string is up, i.e. across the guitar neck towards you as opposed to bending downwards by pushing the string away from you. Bend upwards unless otherwise instructed.

The amount of bending, i.e. the pitch to which the string should be raised is firstly, a musical decision and secondly, a practical one.

Can the string be physically bent that far?

Obviously the heavier the string gauge the greater the tension and the more difficult it becomes to bend a particular string. However, the higher up the neck you play, the closer the frets become and the easier it is to make a bend over a given interval.

In the following examples the 2nd and 3rd strings are used to demonstrate bends from an interval of a semitone (½ tone bend equivalent to 1 fret) to a major 3rd (2 tone bend equivalent to 4 frets). The music displays two notes, the first note (called a grace note) is bent up to the second (principal) note of a designated time value (crotchet, minim etc.).

There is no need to anticipate the bend before the beat. The grace note is played **on the beat** and the bend occurs as quickly as is convenient. The exact speed is dependent upon the tempo and style of the music as well as the player's 'feel'.

In each case the string in question is bent upwards across the guitar neck to the desired pitch.

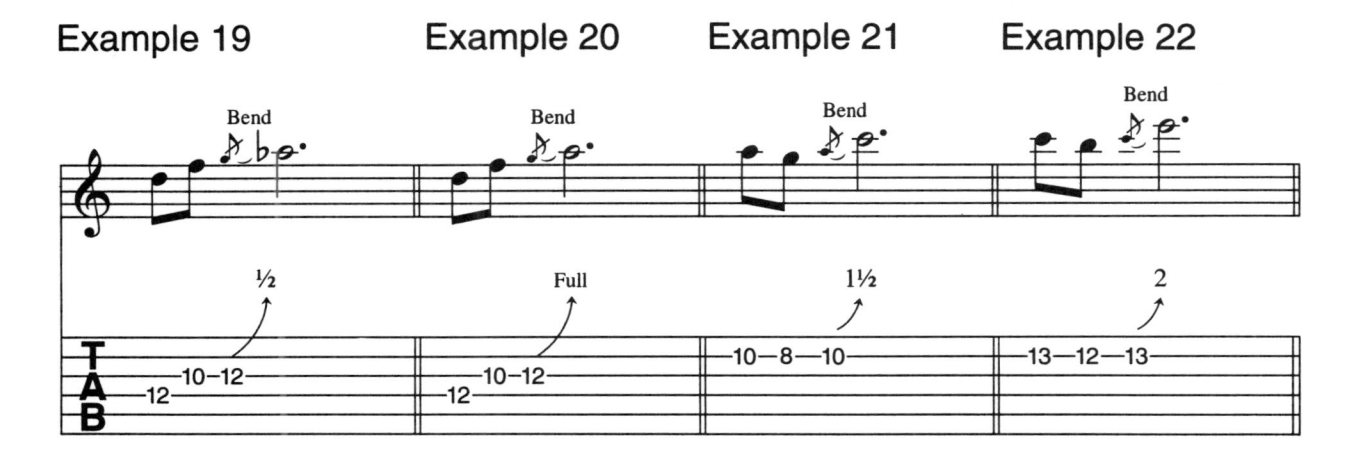

Example 19    Example 20    Example 21    Example 22

A **'decorative' bend** is an embellishment given to a note which requires the pitch of the note to be fractionally raised by a ¼ tone.

In contrast with the previous bends the ¼ tone bend does not attempt to establish a definite new pitch.

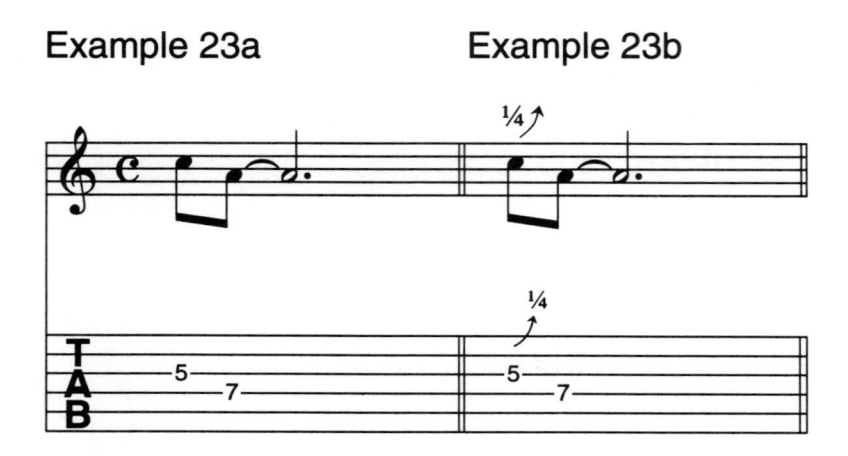

Example 23a          Example 23b

**Pre-bend** *abbr.* Pre, sometimes referred to as a ghost bend.

Besides bending from one note up to another, the already bent note can be released and allowed to fall back to its original pitch. i.e. the note is bent first and then struck on the second pitch. Where the release of the bend starts and finishes is indicated by the time value of the two notes in question. The rate of the release depends on the tempo of the music as well as the individual's interpretation.

To perform a **pre-bend**, bend the string as indicated (i.e. a half or full tone), strike the string and release to the pitch of the second note.

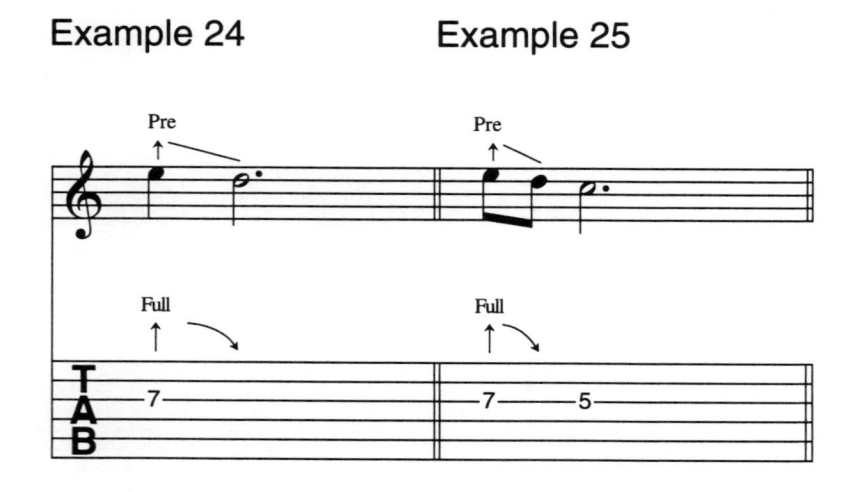

Example 24          Example 25

The **bend and release** of a note can be performed in various ways.

i) In the example that follows the first note is hit and bent as indicated, i.e. the grace note (G) is played on the beat and immediately bent up to the A (full tone bend) and held for three beats before being released again onto the fourth beat whereby the G is re-struck.

With the second example, the first note (G) is bent to the A over a period of a crotchet beat and held for two beats before being released on the fourth beat whereby the G is played.

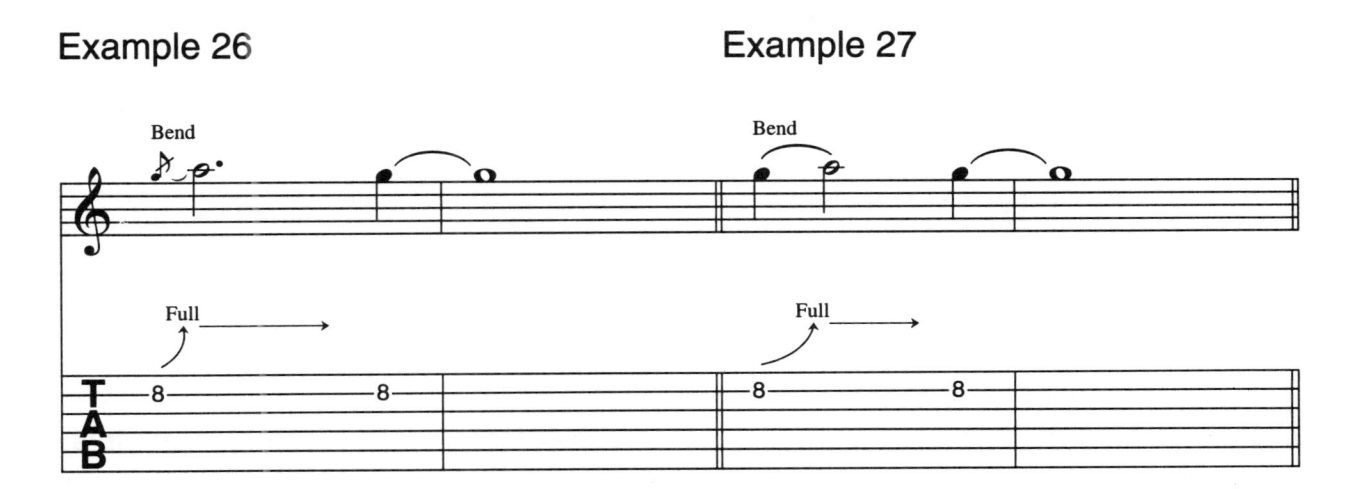

Example 26                                    Example 27

ii) The **bend and release** of a note can also be combined into a single action by striking the string, bending it as directed and then releasing the bend **without** striking the string for a second time. As in the previous example, the speed of the bend (and release) is determined by the time values of the notes in the phrase.

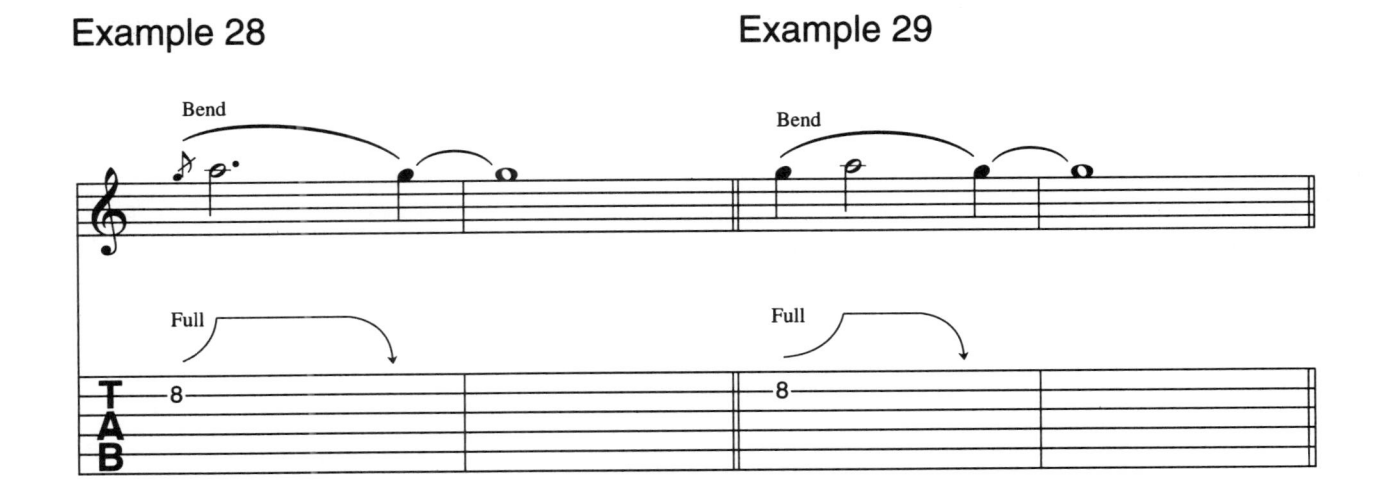

Example 28                                    Example 29

iii) This idea can be taken further by repeating the process of a bend followed by a release without re-striking the string. (Obviously the string has to sustain over this length of time to be able to do this!) The vibrato type effect is represented in the following manner:

**Example 30**

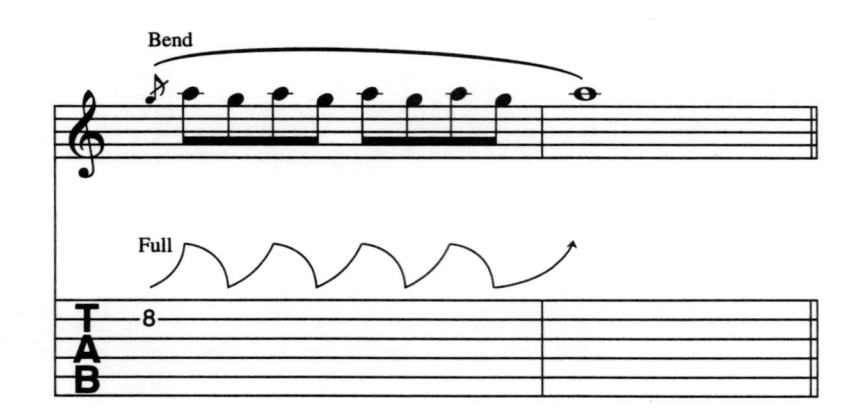

iv) Until now a bend has been created by striking the first note and bending accordingly to the desired pitch. To indicate that the second note of the bend be restruck the symbol ▶ is placed over the note. Compare the difference in notation and effect.

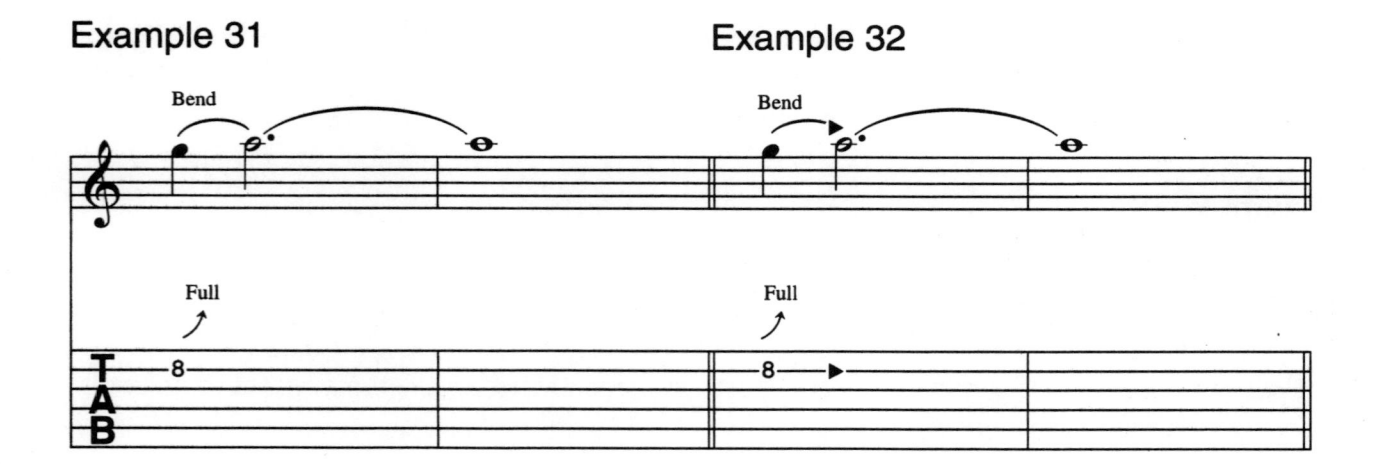

**Example 31**

**Example 32**

**Unison bend** *abbr.* Uni

To play two notes in **unison** is to play the same note on two different strings at the same time. For example, open E on the 1st string played with E on the 5th fret (2nd string).

Similarly the note E played on the 5th fret (2nd string) would be in unison with E on the 9th fret (3rd string) if both strings were played simultaneously.

To create a **unison bend** you need to play the same note simultaneously on adjacent strings by bending the lower string up to the pitch of the top one. In this example the note E is struck on the 2nd string (5th fret) while the D at the 7th fret (3rd string) is bent up a tone (to E), so creating a unison.

Example 33

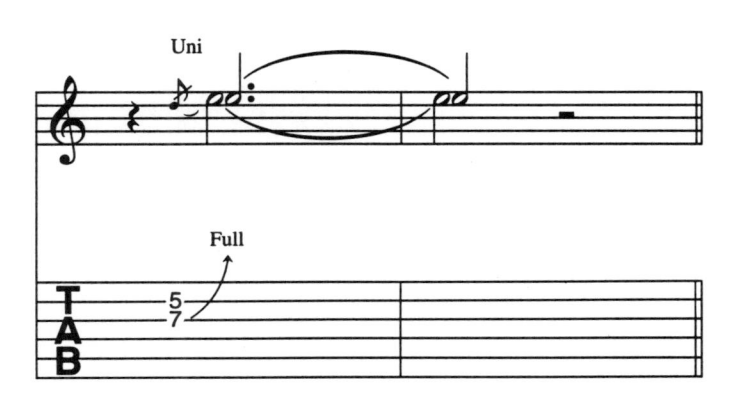

Rather than striking both strings simultaneously, the unison bend can be **'staggered'**, so that the lower note is struck first and bent to the correct pitch. While it is still sounding the higher string is then played. How fast this process occurs is dependent on the time value of each note.

Example 34
Staggered unison bend

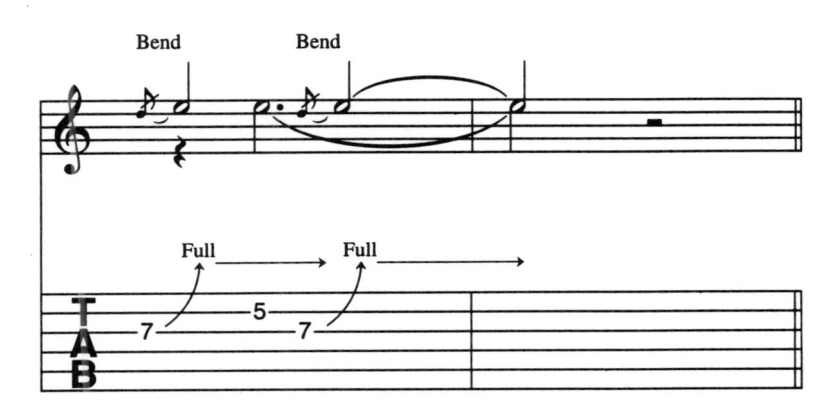

**String bends & vibrato**

The degree to which the string should be bent is generally quite specific (i.e. it is indicated on the music and TAB) but the rate at which this should happen depends on the piece of music and is open to interpretation by the player.

In a similar way the speed and timing of the vibrato is not precisely notated. The sign (〰) does not indicate the rate and depth of the vibrato effect although its time position can be approximately shown by its placement within the music.

In the following examples vibrato is added at various times to the played notes (straight notes and bent notes). The position of the vibrato marking indicates when the effect should begin and end.

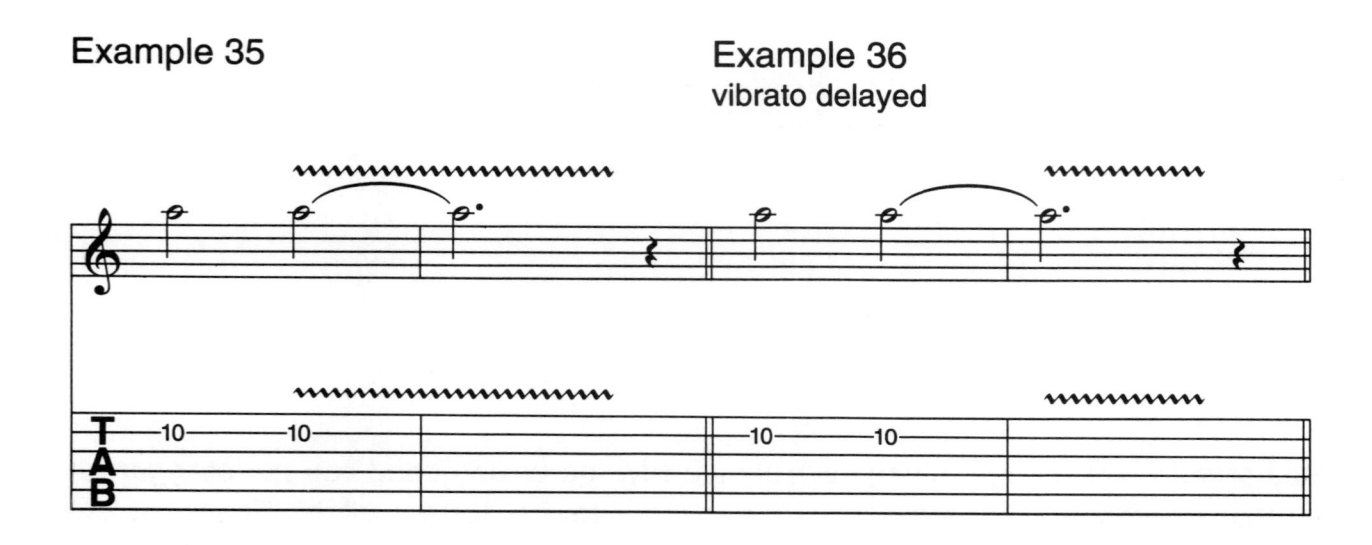

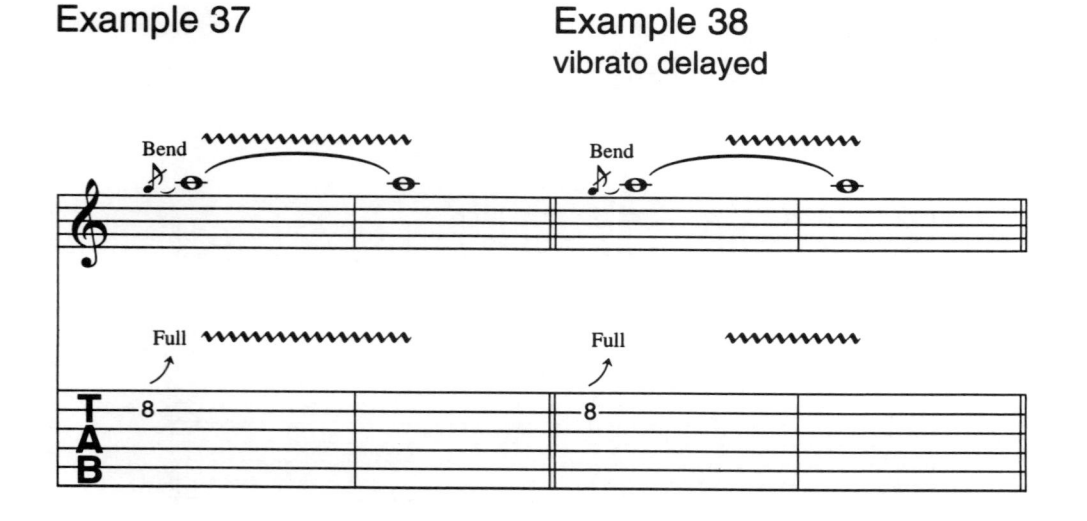

Example 35

Example 36
vibrato delayed

Example 37

Example 38
vibrato delayed

## Musical ornaments – 'hammer–ons and pull–offs'

Rather than striking every note in the phrase (example 39a), the first note (C) is struck, but the following note (D) is played by **hammering** the finger down on the 7th fret without striking the string again. In terms of the fret hand fingering, the first finger frets C at the 5th fret on the 3rd string and the string is played to sound the C note. To play the following note (D) the third finger hammers down onto the 7th fret of the 3rd string.

Compare the following examples.

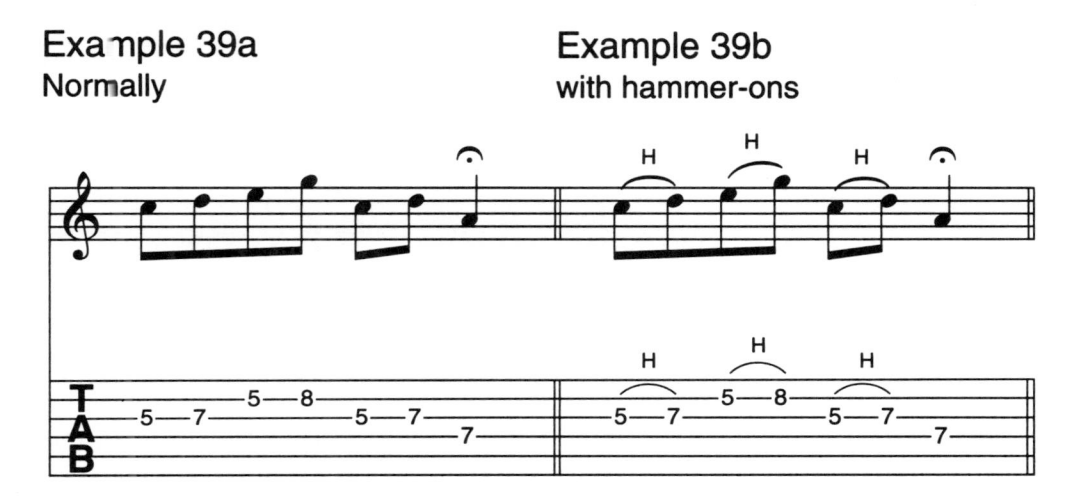

### Example 39a
Normally

### Example 39b
with hammer-ons

The opposite process can be applied to a descending phrase.

The first note (D) is played at the 7th fret on the 3rd string. The third finger which frets the D is then **pulled off** in such a manner as to pluck the C which is being fretted by the first finger at the 5th fret. This is carried out **without** striking the string again.

Try playing the following examples.

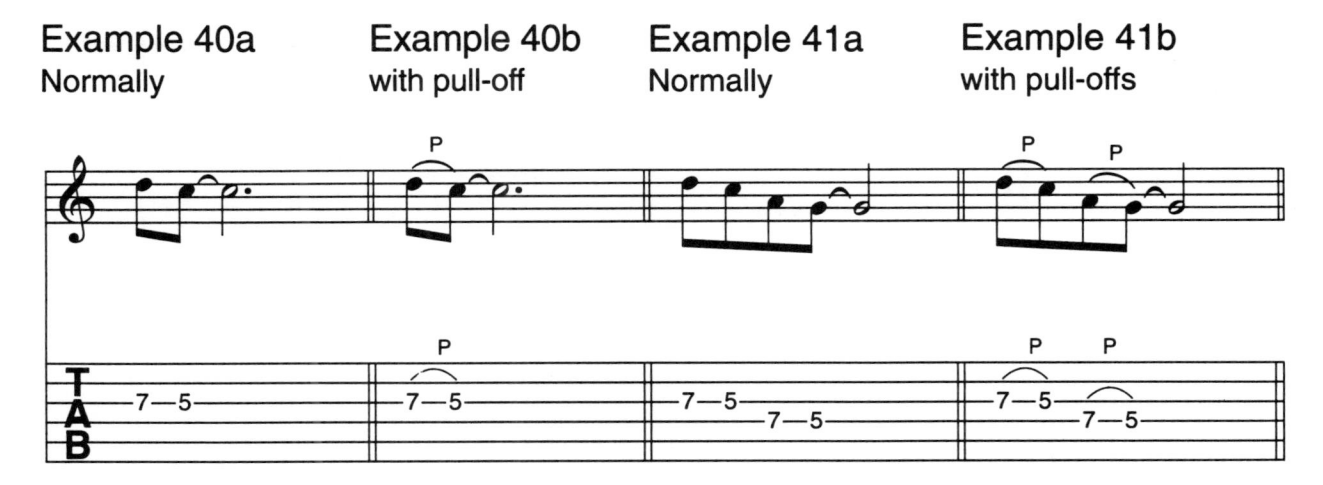

### Example 40a
Normally

### Example 40b
with pull-off

### Example 41a
Normally

### Example 41b
with pull-offs

Hammer-ons and pull-offs can be applied to a succession of notes in a variety of ways. (Obviously the notes are all played on the same string!)

After the first note has been struck the notes that follow may be played by a repetition of hammer-ons and pull-offs.

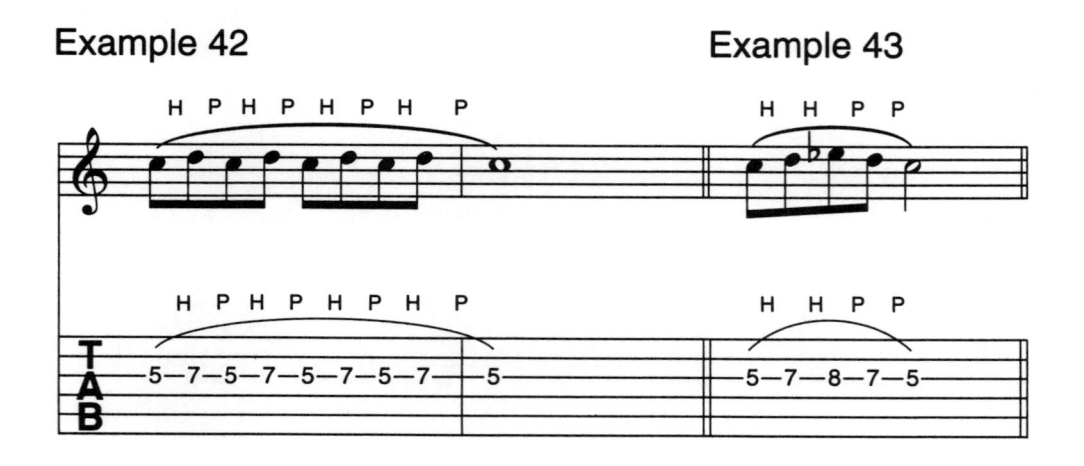

Example 42

Example 43

If the hammer-on/pull-off action is performed fast enough a **trill** effect is produced. The two notes in this action are notated with a trill mark above them (*tr*). If this abbreviation is simply written above a single note it is presumed that the second note of the trill is the next note above in the scale. If this is not the case the two participating notes are written out.

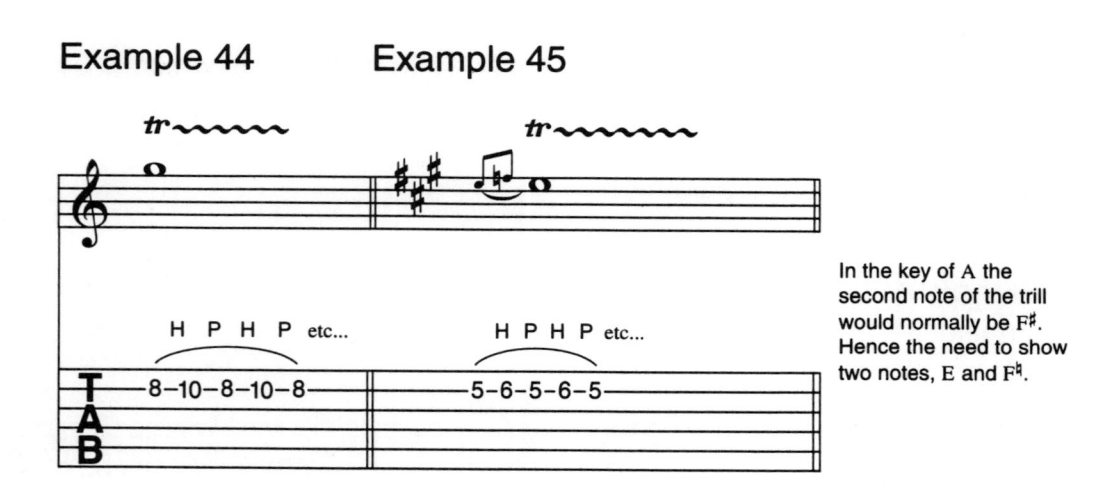

Example 44

Example 45

In the key of A the second note of the trill would normally be F♯. Hence the need to show two notes, E and F♮.

The time values given to each note are directed from the music notation. That is to say the music notation tells us where in the bar each note lies. In addition to these familiar time values (crotchet, quaver etc.) there are further musical ornaments which can be attached to a note.

Most of these ornaments are performed using hammer-ons and pull-offs.

i) We have already mentioned the 'grace' note (the acciaccatura) which is played on the beat as quickly as is convenient. In Example 46 the A will be struck on the beat and quickly pulled-off to play the G. In a similar fashion the opposite can be performed, i.e. the G is played on the beat followed by hammering down on the A.

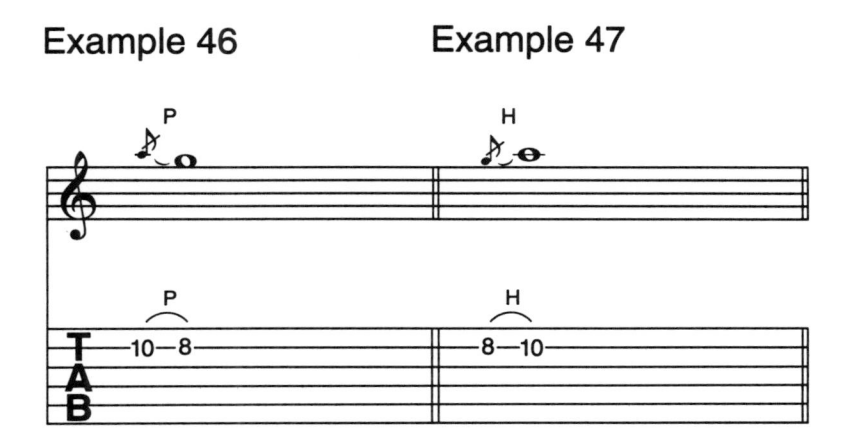

Example 46

Example 47

ii) The **upper mordent** (written as 𝄖 above or below a note) is played by first striking the principal note and then hammering-on to the next note above in the scale followed by an immediate pull-off back to the original note. This is performed as fast as is conveniently possible but consistent with the tempo and style of the music. It is always played on the beat.

Example 48

An accidental above the sign affects the auxiliary note e.g.:

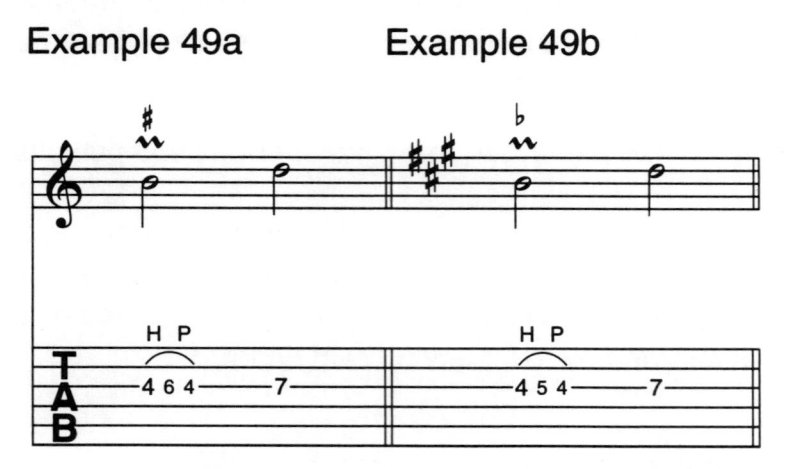

**Example 49a**     **Example 49b**

In the key of A the next note of the scale would be C♯. The ♭ sign now instructs that C♮ is the auxiliary note.

iii) The **lower mordent** is performed in a similar manner but the auxiliary note is now below the principal note.

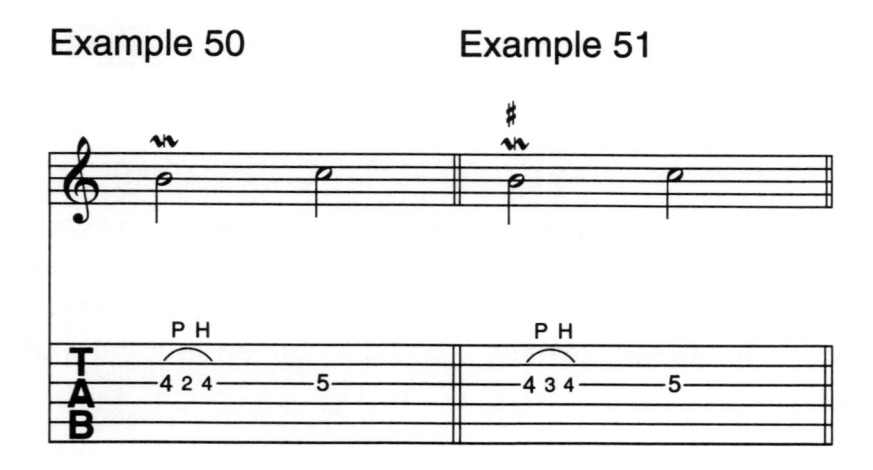

**Example 50**     **Example 51**

There are other ornaments (turn, inverted turn, appoggiatura) which are performed using the hammer-on/pull-off action. For further details, please refer to one of the music theory books available from the Music Sales catalogue.

iv) **Tapping** requires the first note (above which a T is written) to be played by striking the string with the side of the plectrum (or finger) over the fret indicated in the TAB.

In Example 52 the G is sounded by striking the 3rd string at the 12th fret by a plucking action created using either the side of the plectrum or finger.

The next note (B) is then sounded by a pull-off action between the 12th fret (covered by the pick hand) and the 4th fret (fretted by the first finger, fret hand). The note (C) that follows is played by hammering the second finger down on the 5th fret. Play the phrase slowly at first and build up speed gradually – slow and fast versions are demonstrated on the cassette.

Example 52

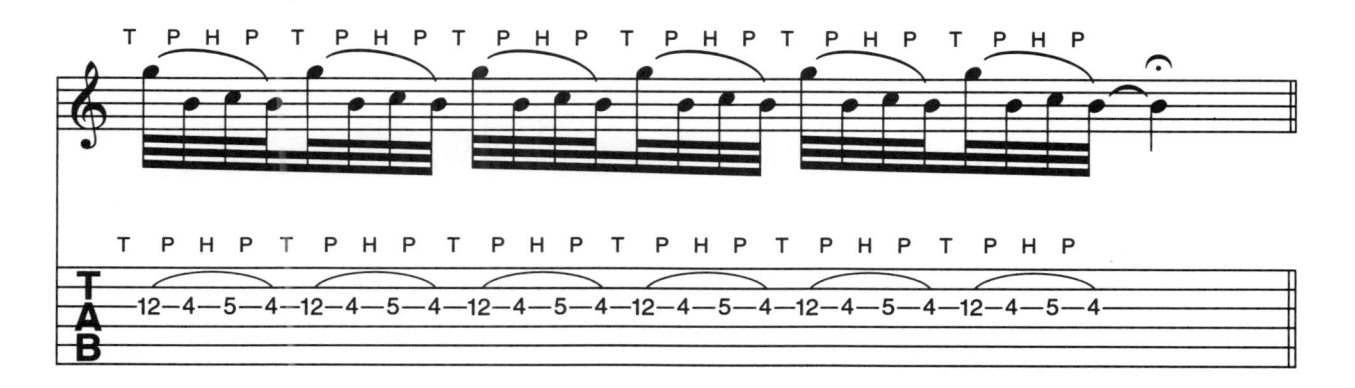

(It is better to have a responsive guitar sound to help produce the desired effect e.g. with sustain/overdrive.)

**Raking** across the strings is a perfect description as the plectrum (or finger) is literally raked across the strings. The effect is of a controlled strum upwards (or downwards) across the strings creating a fast arpeggio.

The resonance of the strings can be regulated by the palm of the pick hand partially covering the strings as they are played. This **damping** or **palm mute** produces a staccato effect. The more the strings are damped the shorter the notes become.

The strings can be totally muted by a combination of the right hand partially covering the strings and the fret hand covering the fret(s) but not actually pressing the string down. This produces a non-pitched percussive sound.

The following examples over the page demonstrate some of the possibilities.

Example 53
Rake up

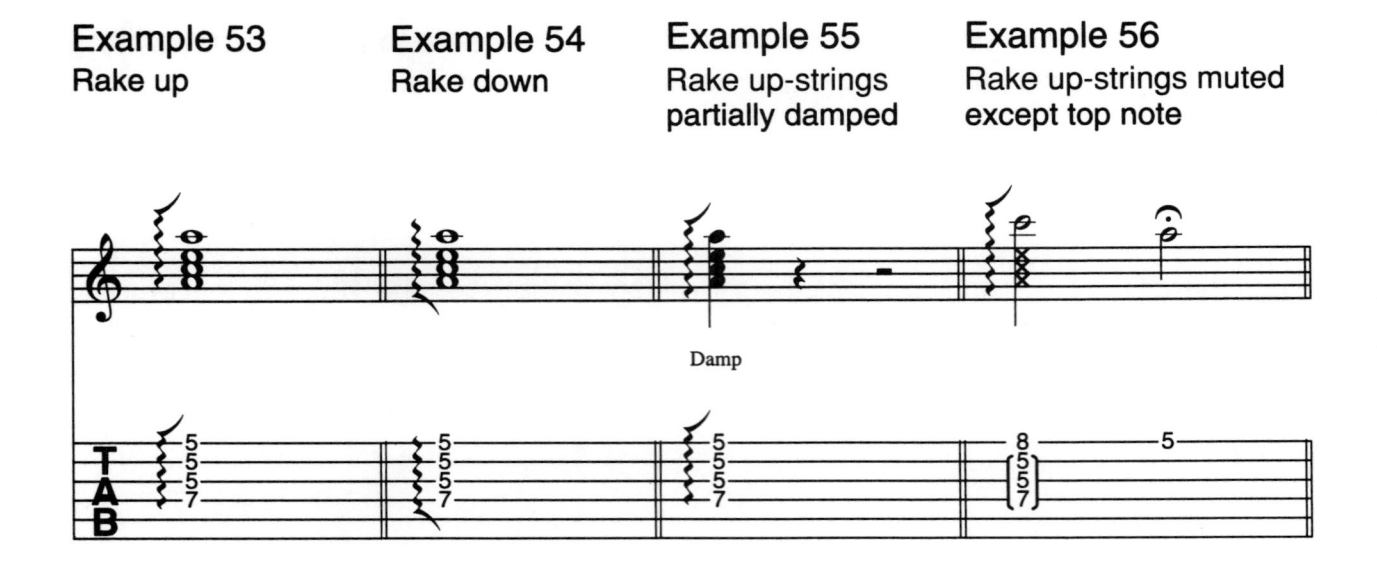

Example 54
Rake down

Example 55
Rake up-strings
partially damped

Example 56
Rake up-strings muted
except top note

Damp

**Harmonics** can be created naturally or artificially.

The natural harmonics are played on the open strings and occur at the 'nodes' of the instrument (i.e. the fractional points across the vibrating length of the strings). At these points the harmonic is sounded by gently placing the fret hand over the actual fret (not the space between the frets as if sounding a note proper) and striking the appropriate string. The most useful natural harmonics can be found at the 12th and 7th frets.

Examples at the 12th fret.

Example 57

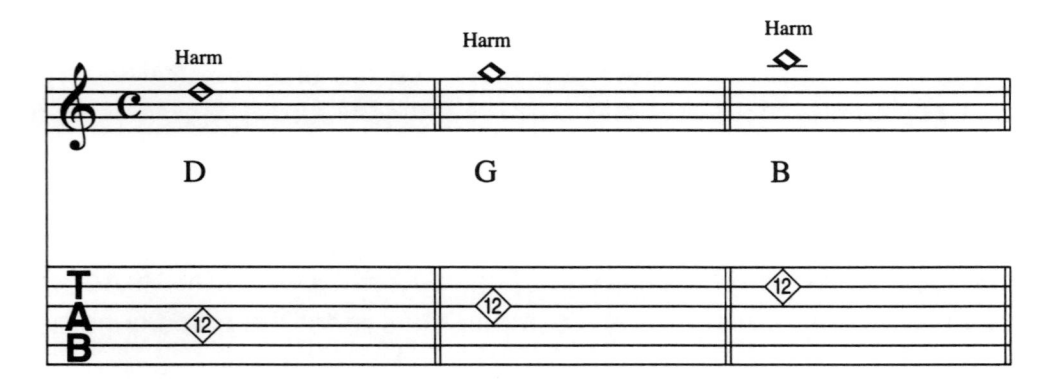

Harm   Harm   Harm

D      G      B

Examples at the 7th fret. (The harmonics created at this position sound an octave higher than the fretted note.)

Example 58

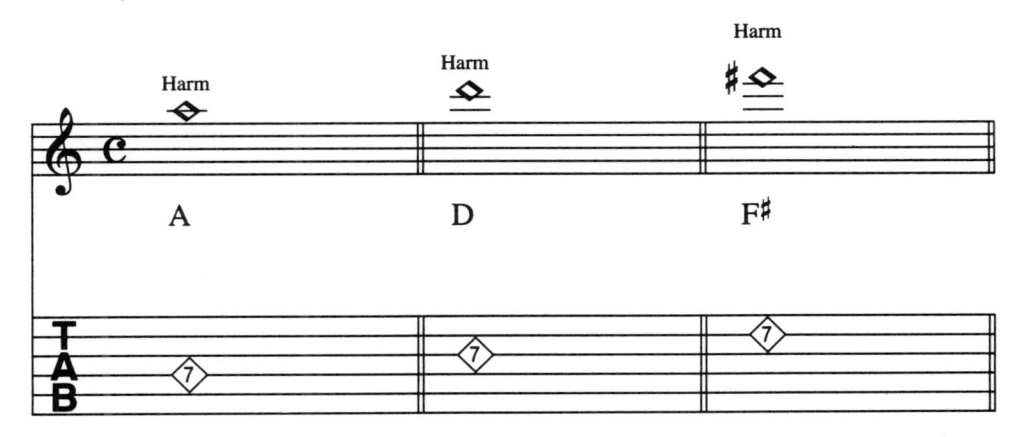

Artificial harmonics are created from a stopped (i.e. fretted) string. The harmonic is played by picking and plucking the string in a kind of pinching action an octave – 12 frets – above the note that is being fretted.

E.g. For example: play a G chord using artificial harmonics.

If the G is fretted at the 5th fret, 4th string, its artificial harmonic can be played at the 17th fret, 4th string. Similarly the harmonic for B at the 4th fret, 3rd string, will be found at the 16th fret, 3rd string, and the harmonics for B and G will be played at the 15th fret and the 2nd and 1st strings respectively.

Example 59

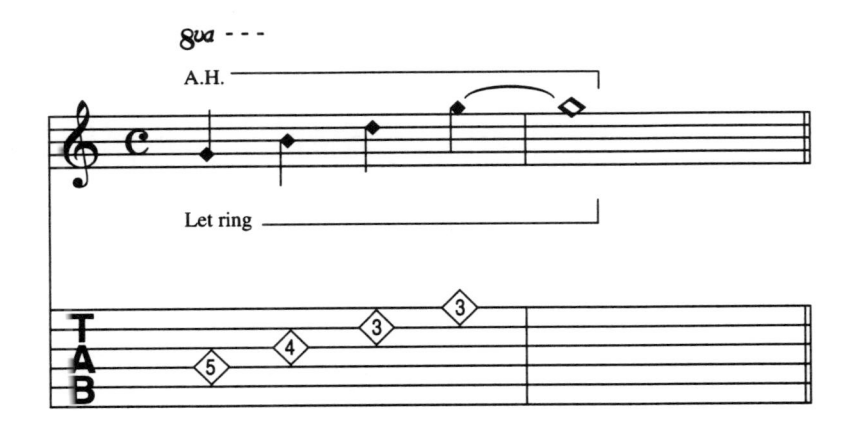

# 10 'Til 2

*by Arthur Dick*

© Copyright 1993 Arthur Dick. Sole printing rights held by Music Sales Limited,
8/9 Frith Street, London W1V 5TZ throughout the World.
All Rights Reserved. International Copyright Secured.

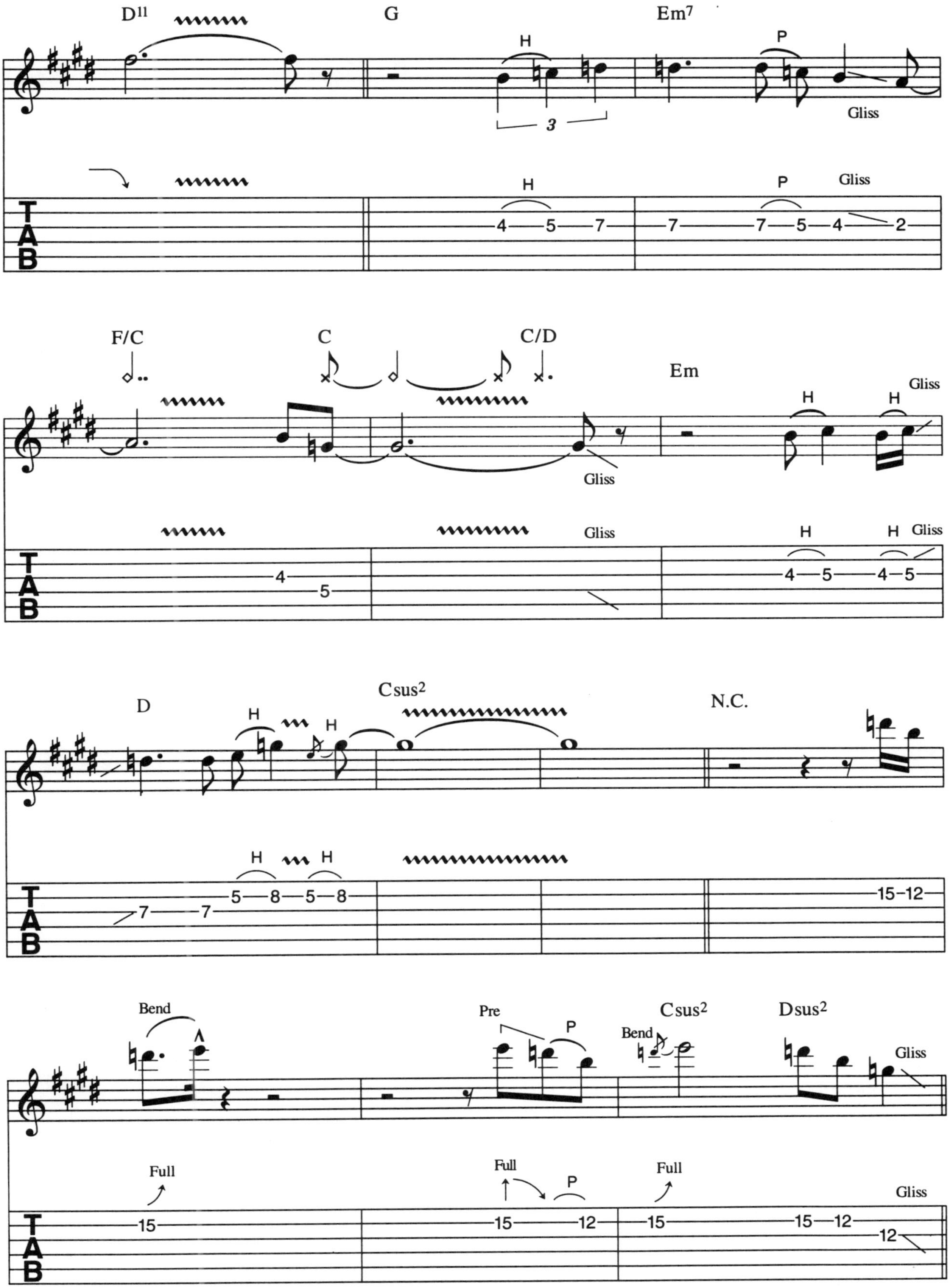

28

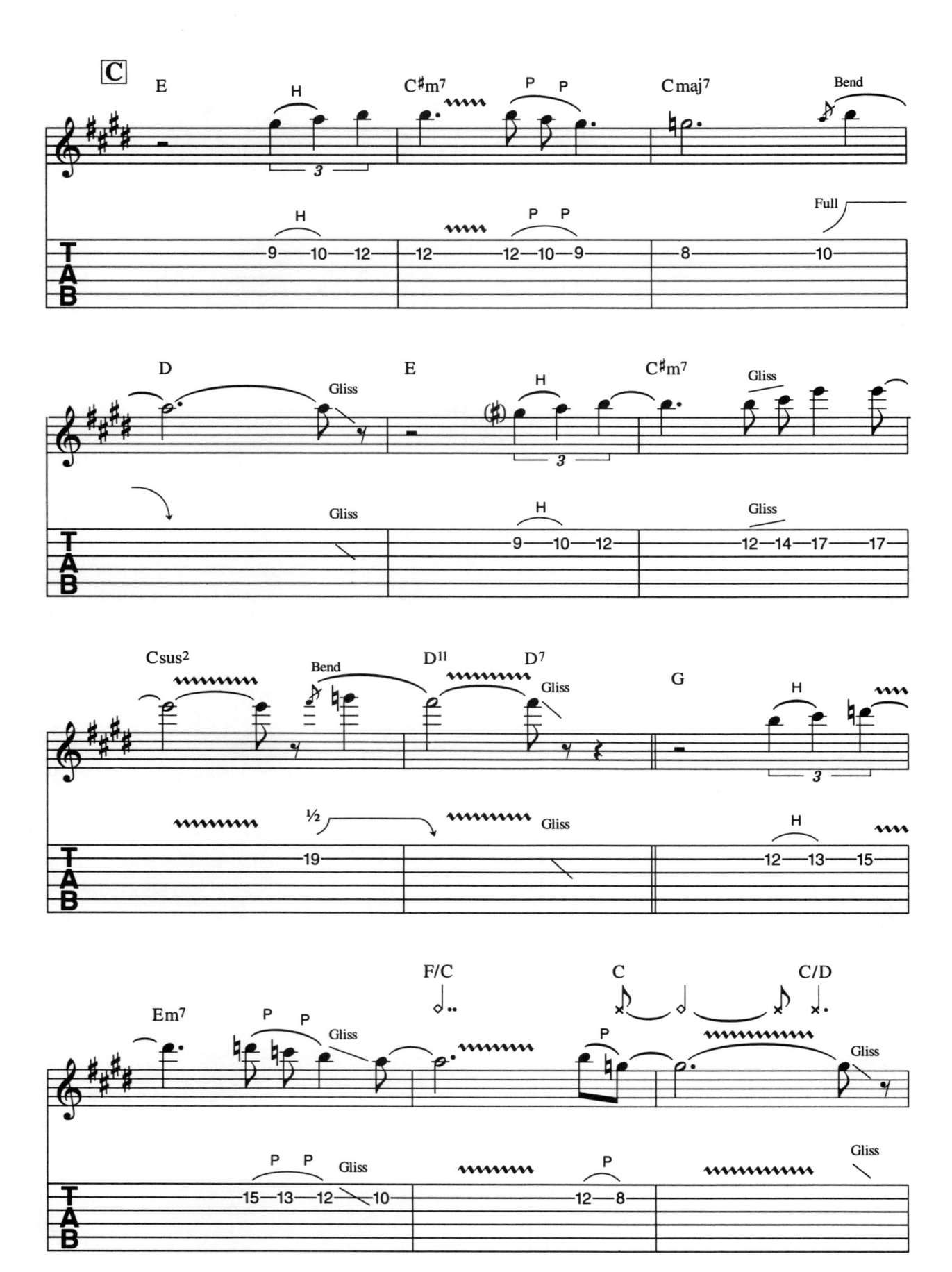

Em
D
Csus2
H
Gliss
Bend
Full
D
N.C.
8
(Whammy bar)
-½
Uni
Release bend
P
Cadd9
Dadd9
¼

E
E
C♯m7
Cmaj7
H
P
Bend
Full
T
A
B
D
E
C♯m7
Gliss
Csus2
D11
D7
G
8va
½
3
Em7
8va (Cont)
F/C
C
C/D
P
Bend

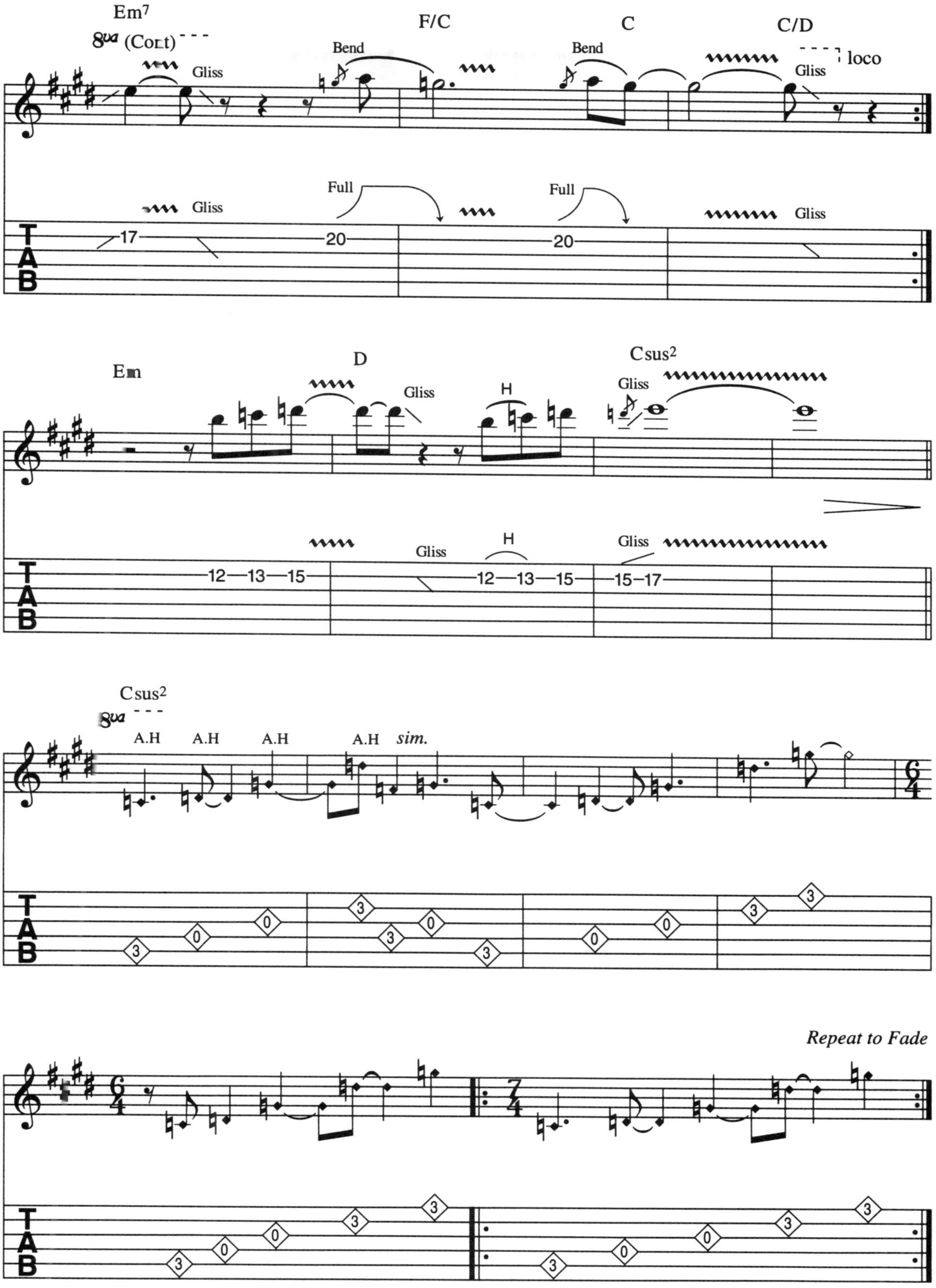
Em7
8va (Cont)
Gliss
F/C
Bend
Full
C
C/D
loco
17
20
Em
D
Csus2
H
12—13—15
15—17
A.H
sim.
Repeat to Fade

There are many musical instructions that can accompany a piece of music. Many of them are Italian words indicating expression as well as general directions to the performer.

| | |
|---|---|
| (♩) | ghost note; a very quiet or nearly silent note |
| > | accent; this symbol appears above notes which should be accented |
| V | Roman numerals above the music notation indicate the position of the fret hand index finger |
| CV | full barré; Roman numerals indicate correct fret |
| ½CV | half barré; Roman numerals indicate correct fret |
| ♩ = 72 | tempo is instructed as 72 crotchet beats per minute |
| *ad lib.* | the speed and interpretation is left to the discretion of the performer |
| **rit.** | abbreviation for ritenuto – means hold back |
| **rall.** | abbreviation for rallentando – means slow down |
| *poco a poco* | means gradually; e.g. *poco a poco cresc.* means gradually get louder |
| < | indicates getting louder |
| > | indicates getting quieter |
| N.C. | means no chord |

| Fretboard fingering indicated by: | T = thumb<br>1 = index finger<br>2 = middle finger<br>3 = ring finger<br>4 = little finger (pinky) | Pick hand fingering indicated by: | p = thumb<br>i = index finger<br>m = middle finger<br>a = ring finger |
|---|---|---|---|

Notation using standard musical text and TAB gives you a more complete musical picture but the entire performance can never be precisely written down. The expression and feel can only be partially conveyed on paper.

You have to listen to the original recording of the transcription and relate what you see to what you hear or interpret the written directions as you feel fit. Experience will help – the more you play the better you will get.

However, one Italian direction that is unambiguous is the term *fine*, it means the end!